Dreams I'm Dreamin'

Devotions for Mothers

Kim Boyce

authorHOUSE™

1663 LIBERTY DRIVE, SUITE 200
BLOOMINGTON, INDIANA 47403
(800) 839-8640
WWW.AUTHORHOUSE.COM

First published by AuthorHouse 08/29/05

ISBN: 1-4208-5729-0 (sc)

Printed in the United States of America
Bloomington, Indiana

This book is printed on acid-free paper.

Dreams I'm Dreamin'

is dedicated to my son,
Alexander Boyce Koreiba.
Your presence in my womb during
the writing of this book provided
inspiration and emotion.
Your daddy, mommy and big brother
are glad Jesus gave you to us.
You are a dream come true!

Contents

Forward by Gigi Graham Tchividjian   ix

Introduction   xi

Dreams I'm Dreamin'

Dreams I'm Dreamin'   3

The Angel and the Music Box   5

Good Job, Mom   7

Hurricane Christina   9

Amazing Love for Me

Amazing Love for Me   15

Fever Seizure   17

Who Hung The Moon?   20

Vibia Perpetua   22

Let's Stay Together

Let's Stay Together   27

Mayhem at McDonald's   29

Date Night   31

Old Mr. Hoover   33

Not Too Far From Here

Not Too Far From Here   39

Homeless in Beverly Hills   42

The Ministry of Compassion   45

I Call Her Blessed   47

The Wise Man Built His House Upon The Rock

The Wise Man Built His House Upon the Rock   53

This Too Shall Pass   55

Grass Soup   58

A Smart Mouth   60

A Man of God   62

My Sweetie Pie

My Sweetie Pie   67

The Jerk at Walt Disney World   69

You're the Boss   71

A Time to Laugh   73

Learn to Live With It   75

Mirror of the Heart

Mirror of the Heart   81

Wonder Woman   84

Walking in His Steps   87

A Wise Woman   89

The Hard Makes it Great   91

I Fall In Love

I Fall In Love   95

Megan and the Puppy   98

Forget the Housework   101

Pass It On   104

Come Home, It's Suppertime   106

Family Prayer   109

Epilogue   111

Acknowledgements   113

Forward

As I read *Dreams I'm Dreamin'*, I was reminded of the many seasons of motherhood that I experienced with my own family. There were times when I was so tired that I didn't think I could go on . . . and yet somehow I was revived by small hands reaching up for a hug, a sticky kiss planted on my cheek, or a young artist's drawing tacked to my refrigerator.

One of the things I appreciate about this book is the way Kim integrated her experiences with Scriptural truth. As a young mother, I was often overwhelmed by the frustrations of running my hectic household; time and again I found the Scriptures to be an unfailing source of guidance and encouragement.

As a grandmother several times over, I want to encourage you to enjoy your children and to treat them as the Lord treats us. Remember the words of King David concerning his own son Solomon:

> *Prayers shall be made for him continually,*
> *and daily shall he be praised.*
>
> PSALM 72:15, KJV

Reading these pages, may you find encouragement in the knowledge that others have been where you are now. Time passes so quickly, and as I look back I am amazed that I survived the experience. And yet, there are moments when I long for those days once more. You will, too – so enjoy them while they last!

Gigi Graham Tchividjian

Introduction

Mothers accomplish a divine purpose. There is no more noble or important occupation than molding the lives of the children God has entrusted to our care. *Dreams I'm Dreamin'* was written to give busy moms, grandmothers, and all those who love children, a chance to sit down for a few minutes, read a chapter or two, and come away with a bit of inspiration. My hope is that each chapter will provide a thought or principle that you can reflect on as you go about your busy day.

This is the second edition of *Dreams I'm Dreamin'*. When I originally wrote the book, my oldest son was three years old, and I was pregnant with my second son. As of this writing, they are eleven and seven. I considered updating the stories and cover photo, but as a sentimental mom, I couldn't bring myself to do it. And since the principles presented in the stories are not changed with the passing of time, I have left the text in its original form.

My prayer is that we all enjoy the children God has given us. As my grandmother told me once, "It doesn't matter if your children have gray hair...they're still your children!" If this little book can bring a laugh, a chuckle, or a tear through the process, then *Dreams I'm Dreamin'* will have done its job.

Kim Boyce
Branson, MO
July, 2005

There is no influence so powerful as that of the mother.

Sarah Josepha Hale

Dreams I'm Dreamin'

Love's greatest mystery has now created you
I wonder for a moment can this be true?
A gift from heaven has touched me somehow
And so I'll start to tell you now

Here is your daddy, the man I love so
He's told you in a whisper, wants you to know
He will protect you, never neglect you
This is a love that daddies know

Dreams I'm Dreamin'
Lullabies I'll be singing
When your little face I see
Hopes I'm hoping
All the prayers I'm praying
Baby, hurry now to me

Have you heard me when I'm asking for Jesus
To make you whole, to watch you grow?
I pray someday His Love you'll know

Dreams I'm dreamin'
Lullabies I'll be singing
When your little face I see
Hopes I'm hoping
All the prayers I'm praying
Baby, hurry now to me

Dreams I'm Dreamin'

For You have formed my inward parts;
You have covered me in my mother's womb.
I will praise You, for I am fearfully and wonderfully made.

PSALM 139:13-14A

I wrote the lyrics to "Dreams I'm Dreamin'" when I was three months pregnant with my son, Gary Lee Koreiba II. I was so excited about all of the wonderful experiences that my husband Gary and I were going to have with this child. And like most first-time parents, we never imagined that there would be anything except happiness, laughter and joy associated with our child. Boy, did we have a lot to learn!

After a few sleepless nights, unexplained crying sessions (by the baby *and* me!) and experiencing that sinking "what-in-the-world-have-we-gotten-ourselves-into" feeling, reality began to set in. I was suddenly faced with the fact that my child was going to cry, spit up, poop and *not* sleep just like all of those other people's kids who were so badly behaved.

Within a few days, though, things didn't look quite so bleak. I found out that I could actually survive on a couple of hours sleep here and there. I figured out the difference between the hungry cry, the dirty diaper cry, the "you're not holding me right" cry and the "just-needing-a-good-cry" cry. And I also learned – for the first time in my life – what true selflessness was all about.

My son has continued to teach me many lessons. And all of that joy, happiness and laughter that I had dreamed of has come along with him, too. Sure, there are the days when I would like to have a little time to myself, but then I remember how much I hated being single and alone in my mid-twenties, and how I would dream of having all of the things that I have now. Even on the hardest days, I wouldn't trade my incredible husband and son for anything.

Maybe I'm glutton for punishment, but as I sit writing today, I'm three months pregnant with my second child. So I'm dreaming those dreams all over again!

Heavenly Father,
Thank You for my wonderful family. Even though we are
not perfect, I praise You for this group of people that You
have ordained as those who will be closest to me. Help
me to be the best wife, mother and woman that I can be
– today and every day of my life. Amen.

The Angel and the Music Box

For He shall give His angels charge over thee,
to keep thee in all thy ways.

PSALM 91:11, KJV

My sister-in-law Maralee and her husband Dennis had put their two-year-old son to bed with a cold. Nothing unusual, just the run-of-the-mill childhood cold. To help Aaron breathe, Maralee had turned on the vaporizer in her son's room before going to bed herself.

A couple of hours later, Dennis was awakened by a strange sound. The music box in Aaron's room was playing. Dennis got out of bed to investigate. Why would it suddenly be playing in the middle of the night?

As he walked down the hall toward Aaron's bedroom, Dennis remembered that the music box only played if the drawer inside it was pulled completely open. The sense that something was wrong grew stronger.

Quickly he opened Aaron's door. Sparks were flying from the electrical outlet where the vaporizer was plugged in. As he hurried to unplug the unit, Dennis realized that, had the music box not started playing, he would never have know anything was wrong.

In the dim light that filtered in from the hallway, Dennis looked at the music box on his son's dresser. The drawer was closed. There was no reason the music box should have been playing. No natural reason, anyway.

I've often wondered what song the music box in Aaron's bedroom played. Maybe *"All night, all day. Angels watching over me, my Lord. All night, all day. Angels watching over me."*

This story of supernatural intervention has been a comfort to me since I first heard it. I remember it when I become fearful of all of the terrible things that could happen to my son. From sickness, to tragedy, to kidnapping – whenever these things run through my mind, it helps to know that angels are guarding my son and that his life is in God's care.

When fear begins to rob us of our joy, it's time to go to our loving Savior and ask for the peace that only He can give.

Heavenly Father,
I pray for Your protection upon my children. Cover them with the blood of Jesus and keep them in Your care. Give me peace to rest in Your love, and ever remind me that You have not given me a spirit of fear but of power, love and a sound mind (see 2 Timothy 1:7). Amen.

Good Job, Mom

Even a child is known by his deeds,
By whether what he does is pure and right.

PROVERBS 20:11

This morning I have been involved in the very important work of taping the covers back onto the pages of my son's books. He somehow manages to disconnect the front and back covers of most of his books as he scurries from place to place, scattering them as he goes. So "book doctoring" is a significant project.

I'll never forget the first time he noticed what I had done to his books. "Good job, Mom," he said. It made my whole day.

Now he says this to me when I cook a dinner that he particularly enjoys, if I've opened the lid of a container that he was unable to open himself or drawn an especially good train in his art book, and for various other reasons that he feels deserve to be complimented.

Little Gary is generous with his praise because he has been taught this trait. His daddy says, "Good job, Mom," after dinner, so he does, too. When Gary has been up on the roof cleaning out the gutters, he comes down and I say, "Good job, Dad," so Little Gary repeats the compliment.

Children learn by example. We can tell them to be kind and good, but if they don't see us model kindness and goodness, they won't know how to become kind and good themselves. In fact, you can *tell* your children to do virtuous things all day long, but if they don't see them portrayed, the message will not get through.

As parents, we must be convinced of our beliefs. We must know where we stand, so that our children will know where *they* stand. I'm hoping that one day when my son is grown, he will look back and appreciate the values and beliefs that Gary and I have taught him. Then maybe I'll hear my favorite of compliments: "Good job, Mom!"

Heavenly Father;
Thank You for the opportunity to teach my children the
beliefs and values I hold dear. Remind me daily of the
responsibilities I have in bringing up my children in "the
training and admonition of the Lord" (Ephesians 6:4).
Amen.

Hurricane Christina

And suddenly there came a sound from heaven,
as of a rushing mighty wind, and it filled
the whole house where they were sitting.

ACTS 2:2

Now I *know* this scripture is referring to the day of Pentecost and the arrival of the Holy Spirit, but I can think of no better way to describe a new baby's arrival. The new sounds seem to rush through and fill the whole house! Perhaps no couple has experienced the literal merging of a new baby and the rushing mighty wind quite like my sister Tina and my brother-in-law Larry.

Tina and Larry's second child, Christina, joined her mom, dad, and brother Chad in September 1989 in Charlotte, North Carolina. Just as Tina, Larry and my mom (who was in town to help with the new arrival) brought Christina home from the hospital, a hurricane struck. Electrical power was lost, so for a few days my sister's family experienced life like the pioneers. When Tina had problems nursing Christina, Larry had to light the gas grill outside to boil water to make bottled formula. When Christina awoke in the middle of the night for a feeding, there were no lights, so they used candles. Cooking meals was impossible, so the rest of the family had to snack on whatever was available until Larry could light the grill again.

I guess you could say that this hurricane was a sign of things to come. It seems to fit Christina's personality that she arrived amidst such a phenomenon. Chad had always been a perfect child. My sister admits that she has never had more than a moment's trouble with her son. Her mothering skills got a little more testing with Christina.

Now, don't get me wrong. Christina was not a demon or a hooligan, but she was *normal*. She was rambunctious and rowdy, she liked to test her boundaries, and she still has a strong will...all very normal. And I'm so glad. You see, if my sister and Larry had produced another "perfect child," I would have thought they had abnormal genes or something.

I'm also very happy that Christina has the personality she does because it's consoling to me. My son has the very same personality. Christina is older now, and I can see that she is a well-behaved, intelligent child. And because of her, I can see clearly how certain traits that cause me anxiety with my son right now will someday turn into positive characteristics that will serve him well later in life.

I suppose every mother has her doubts as to how to best raise a child. Each child's personality is different, so we must prayerfully consider how to handle each child in a unique and special way. Maybe my second child will be a sedate, calm, pliable soul who will sleep through the night from day one, but I'm not holding my breath. Besides, I wouldn't trade my first little hurricane for anything!

In raising children, all you can do is your best...We take care of the possible and leave the impossible to God.

Ruth Bell Graham

Heavenly Father,
Thank You for the unique personalities that You have given
to each and every child. Help me to discover each talent
and gift with which You have blessed my children, and
may I learn how to best cultivate each of the blossoms You
have planted within their souls. Amen.

Amazing Love for Me

I've heard the story since I was a child myself
How You watched from above as the son that you loved
Faced a shameful death
It's always stirred my heart
But lately like I've never known
'Cause now I've felt the joy of holding a son of my own
Oh, Father

How could You turn Him loose
When You knew what was to come?
How could You watch what He went through?
I would've screamed for Him to run
But You set aside Your deepest feelings
To meet my deepest need
How could You have such amazing love for me?

I'd want to shelter my son from this world of pain
Yet before time began the cross was Your plan
And You were silent when it came
There was just one way we could be reconciled
Forgiveness called for holy blood
You offered Your only child
Lord, tell me

How could You turn Him loose
When You knew what was to come?
How could You watch what He went through?
I would've screamed for Him to run
But You set aside Your deepest feelings
To meet my deepest need
How could You have such amazing love for me?

Amazing Love for Me

For God so loved the world that He gave His only begotten Son, that whoever believes in Him should not perish but have everlasting life.

JOHN 3:16

A couple of weeks after our son was born, my in-laws called to check on us. During course of the conversation, they asked Gary, "Now do you see how much we love you?" Gary told me later that at first he thought it was a strange question; he had always known that he was loved.

As we talked about it, though, we realized that we never fully understood how much our parents loved us until we became parents ourselves. As the conversations progressed, we also realized that we never truly knew the depth of God's love for us as His children until our son was born.

God loved us enough to sacrifice His only Son to save us from our sin (see John 3:16). When we became parents, this truth became an overwhelming thought. We knew that we could never give our son's life for someone else. Every parent that we have discussed this with has echoed the same sentiment, so we know that it was truly the divine love of a Heavenly Father that allowed Jesus to die for us.

When I was writing songs for my album "As I Am," I wanted to have a song that would talk about the new appreciation I had for God's generosity. "Amazing Love for Me" was the result. Every time I sing this song, I am once again awestruck by God's unconditional love for me, a sinner. Was my salvation worth the life of God's perfect Son, Jesus? To the Father it was.

Maybe, like me, you had to become a mother to truly understand the immense sacrifice that God made in giving Jesus Christ for your sin. Once you get a glimpse of that kind of love, it changes you forever. Have you ever thanked God for what He did for you and asked Him to be the Lord of your life? If not, this simple prayer is the best place to start:

Heavenly Father,
Thank You for sending Your Son, Jesus Christ, to die for my
sin. Jesus, I believe that You are the Son of God, and I ask
You to come into my heart and be my Savior. I confess my
sin to You and give You control of my life. Thank you for
loving me. Amen.

Fever Seizure

Gracious is the Lord, and righteous;
Yes, our God is merciful

PSALM 116::5

*L*ittle Gary, who was fourteen months old at the time, had come home from our last concert tour with a cold. He was starting to run a fever, so I had called his doctor to find out what to do. The doctor suggested I watch him for a couple of days to see whether he would get any worse or if this particular illness would simply run its course.

Since we had been away from home for awhile, we were running low on food, so I suggested to Gary that we make a quick trip to the grocery store, the drug store and Home Depot to pick up some things that we needed. By the time we reached Home Depot, Little Gary was getting irritable. We put our son into the seat of the shopping cart and went quickly through the store to get what we needed.

I was pushing the cart when I noticed Little Gary fall back in the seat and go limp. I reached down and lifted his head. "Gar-Gar, what's wrong?" His eyes were glazed, and he was completely lethargic and unresponsive. I spoke to him again, then realized what was happening.

"He's having a fever seizure!" I yelled to Gary. "Let's go NOW!"

Grabbing Little Gary out of the cart, we started running. By the time we reached the parking lot, Little Gary was vomiting but was still unresponsive. Instinctively, I started to pray. I prayed like I didn't even know I could pray. As Gary started driving, we realized that Little Gary's doctor's office was *right across the street* from Home Depot. The Lord was watching out for us. It only took us about three minutes to cross the four-lane high- way.

Our wonderful pediatrician, Dr. Henderson, took our son in his arms and began to examine him while asking questions about exactly what had happened. When he fell back in the cart, had Little Gary stiffened up? No. Had he foamed at the mouth? No. The nurse took Little Gary's temperature. It was 105 degrees! Much too high. The first thing we had to do was to get the fever down. Dr. Henderson gave him some type of fever medication and then instructed me to try to get him to drink some cool water.

As Gary and I sat in the examination room holding our whimpering son, we knew that we were helpless. What an awful feeling! After two hours or so, Dr. Henderson explained to us that this was probably an isolated seizure brought on by the rapid ascent of the fever. It didn't appear to be related to a serious illness, such as epilepsy. "The Lord was watching out for this little guy," Dr. Henderson observed.

As I reflect on that terrible day, I *know* that God was watching out for my son. Not only were we across the street from the doctor's office, but just the night before I had read about fever seizures in a children's health book. Had I not read that section of the book, I wouldn't have known what was happening, nor would I have appreciated the seriousness of the situation.

It's been an amazing thought to realize that God cares so much for my family that He orchestrated the little "miracles" that occurred that day. He cares about every part of our lives, big or small, because we're *His* children. Isn't that amazing love?

Heavenly Father,

Thank You for caring about every area of my life. Thank You for Your protection over the lives of my children. Allow me to rest in the knowledge of your care. Amen.

Who Hung The Moon?

In the beginning God created the heavens and the earth.

One night when Little Gary was two years old, we were going out someplace. As I was opening the car door, he looked up at the night sky and said, "Mommy, look at the stars!"

I quickly glanced up, expecting to give it a passing "Oh, yeah," but I was struck by the beauty of the blackened sky illuminated with millions of tiny lights. I looked down at my son, who was still mesmerized by the sight. A tiny child's eyes made me see the beauty in God's creation. If I had been by myself that evening, I probably would never have noticed the magnificence high above me.

Because of Little Gary, I again see things I haven't really *seen* for years ... a ladybug on the sidewalk, gold-fish in a pond, birds outside our windows, those little weeds that send furry white particles flying when you blow on them. It's such a pleasure to enjoy the awesome majesty of nature. God created the beauty of this earth to remind us of Himself. And it took a two-year-old to help me remember.

Little Gary's fascination with creation prompted me to record "Who Hung the Moon?":

When I see my baby smile I realize that life's
   worthwhile.
How easily can you and me get lost in a hurry.
Stop and take the time to see the miracle of
   creativity.
Just like a breeze fills the air

Could someone be out there?
Why do stars come out at night?
Just take a look around, don't let it pass you by.
Who hung the moon?
Someone had to plan it, don't take it all for granted
When the stars come out at night.

Man has been interested in God's role as Creator since the beginning of time. Alternate theories of the world's creation abound, but no one has ever come up with a valid, concrete answer as to how the galaxies came to be—apart from God. How can someone look at the majesty of the Rocky Mountains, or the breathtaking beauty of a sunset, or the perfectly formed fingers of a newborn and deny the existence of God? It doesn't make sense that all of this beauty is the result of some cosmic explosion. It can't be explained by saying that some amoeba crawled up onto a prehistoric shoreline, and There we are! No, even creation itself knows who the Creator is.

> *When I consider Your heavens, the work of Your fingers, The moon and the stars which You have ordained, What is man that You are mindful of him, And the son of man that You visit him?*
> *PSALM 8:3-4*

Heavenly Father,
Thank You for the beauty of creation. May it always remind me of You and Your majesty in the earth. Always allow me to sense Your presence in the things You have created. Amen.

Vibia Perpetua

Trust in the Lord with all your heart,
And lean not on your own understanding;
In all our ways acknowledge Him,
And He shall direct your paths.

PROVERBS 3:5

WARNING! Whatever you do, do not finish reading this chapter. Save it for a day when you are feeling sorry for yourself. And even then, only read it if you want a total change of attitude. If this describes you today, then read on...

My friend Kim gave me a book entitled *Great Women of the Christian Faith*. This book has been an inspiration to me, and I highly recommend it—even though I've never actually been able to read the book from cover to cover.

I can never read more than a few chapters at a time. The reason is simple: I feel like such a complete loser when I compare my life with the lives of these women. It takes me a couple of days to recuperate emotionally after reading just the first chapter of the book. And yet it is a beautiful story, and I'd like to share it with you today.

Vibia Perpetua (AD. 181?-203) was of noble birth. She was young, beautiful and educated. As one of the first Christian converts in third-century North Africa, she knew that her faith could cost her everything. Yet Perpetua was willing to face the beasts in the arena rather than renounce her faith in Jesus Christ.

The day came when Perpetua, her maidservant Felicitas and four Christian men were arrested and sent to prison to await trial before the tribunal. While in prison, Perpetua's spirit became burdened, not for herself but (and this is the part that gets me!) for her infant son, whom she had to leave behind.

Through the intercession of two influential men, Perpetua's son was brought to her in prison. Read her words of the experience:

> *I suckled my child, who was already weak from want of nourishment ... and then I obtained leave that my child should remain with me in the prison. Immediately I gained strength and, being relieved of my anxiety about the child, my prison suddenly became to me a palace, so that I preferred to be there rather than anywhere else.*

On the day of their trials, Perpetua and her friends refused to renounce their faith and were sentenced to death in the arena, to be torn apart by wild beasts and then beheaded by the gladiator's sword. When Perpetua and her companions marched into the arena to meet their deaths, they were singing a psalm.

What great faith and courage these early church martyrs possessed! The faith of these men and women touches our lives today, for it is because of Vibia Perpetua and many others like her, who gave their lives for the cause of Christ, that we have heard the Good News.

May the story of the life of Vibia Perpetua help us to put our own lives in perspective. We have so much about which to be thankful. I don't know about you, but after reading about Perpetua, suddenly the trials and 'hardships" of my life don't seem quite so unbearable.

Heavenly Father,
Make my heart trust in You when circumstances cause me
to doubt. Always help me remember that You light my path
and lead my way when I yield control of my life to You.
Amen.

Let's Stay Together

From the moment that I saw you
I knew everything would be so fine
I knew in an instant
Our love had to be divine
Our friendship grew and then love bloomed
You moved me like no other
This love will last
Forget the past
There'll never be another

Why are there always people who say it can't be done
Nothing lasts forever
You better take a look at us

Scarlett and a man named Rhett
Romeo and Juliet
Couldn't keep their love together, no
Let's stay together
Baby, it's up to me and you
Whatever comes we're gonna see it through
And keep our love together, oh
Let's stay together

Seems that everywhere we look around us
Relationships are broken
Giving up on promises and sacred words once spoken
A promise made and then not kept
Not the way we're gonna do it now
You are my hope my treasure
You never let me down…

If your love grows distant,
God's love makes the difference
With His help we'll be together, Baby
Reaffirm my promise I'll be true and honest
I believe in forever

Scarlett and a man named Rhett
Romeo and Juliet
Couldn't keep their love together, no
Let's stay together
Baby, it's up to me and you
Whatever comes we're gonna see it through
And keep our love together, oh
Let's stay together

Let's Stay Together

Therefore a man shall leave his father and mother and be joined to his wife,
and they shall become one flesh.

GENESIS 2:24

One day shortly after we were married, Gary and I started reminiscing about our first school friends wand realized that between the two of us we could only think of three kids whose parents were divorced. I would guess that today you couldn't walk into any elementary school class and find only three children who came from broken homes.

"They shall become one flesh," (Genesis 2:24). Becoming "one flesh" in marriage is one thing. Staying "one flesh" takes work. And a lot of folks just don't want to work that hard. I've become convinced the number one cause of divorce is not adultery or financial problems or emotional distress but selfishness. Scripture is full of exhortations to esteem others more highly than ourselves (Philippians 2:3), love our neighbors (Mark 12:3 1) and look out for the interests of others (Philippians 2:4). And yet many relationships fail because these principles are overlooked.

Now, I'm not suggesting you roll over and play dead. If you are in a physically or emotionally abusive relationship, or if your spouse is committing adultery, then you need to seek professional help immediately, for your own sake as well as for your children's.

On the other hand, most relationships—especially marriages—could benefit from a good dose of selflessness. Try it, and see if yours improves.

What's so remarkable about love at first sight? It's when people have been looking at each other for years that it becomes remarkable.

Anonymous

Heavenly Father,
Help me today to show Your humility in my relationships. Convict me of selfishness in my life and allow me to be "other-centered" rather than self-centered. Strengthen my marriage and my relationship with my children through Your love. Amen.

Mayhem at McDonald's

A merry heart does good, like medicine,
But a broken spirit dries the bones.

PROVERBS 17:22

One of my favorite stories in my family's history occurred when I was four years old and my younger sister, Tina, was two. It was 1965. Mom and Dad loaded us into their white Buick convertible with the red leather interior and took us to the new hamburger joint in town, McDonald's. At that time, McDonald's was only a take-out restaurant, so Dad went up to the window to order our food while Mom, Tina and I waited impatiently in the car.

As Dad was getting into the car with a cardboard tray full of food and drinks, he handed the tray over to my mom, intending for her to take the *entire* tray. Mom thought he wanted her to take *her* drink ... so she did. And by her removing one drink from the carefully balanced tray, the rest of our meals ended up in my dad's lap!

As my sister and I watched in disbelief from the backseat, my dad calmly proceeded to scoop up the remains of his milkshake and throw it right in Mom's face! In complete shock (but not to be outdone), my normally-refined mother took the lid off of her Coke and threw her drink at Dad!

As hilarious as this scene must have been, the best part of the story is what happened next. As Mom wiped milkshake from her face and Dad sat dripping in soda, brushing hamburgers and french-fries off his lap, things could have gotten pretty nasty. But my parents started laughing! No screaming of obscenities, no name-calling. Just laughter.

Imagine what a traumatic experience this could have been for Tina and me had there been screaming, yelling or slapping. We would never have forgotten the sight of our parents in such an altercation. But they laughed! They laughed uncontrollably at themselves and at each other. Really! What else could they have done? Started blaming each other for what had happened? Your credibility in any argument is pretty well shot when you're covered in Coke and milkshake.

Maybe the day will come when you and your husband will be at a crossroads of arguing ridiculously or laughing. Which option will you choose? If there are little eyes watching you, what would you like them to remember about Mom and Dad thirty or so years down the road?

Communicating properly is something that all couples should work on. And just in case all your efforts fail and miscommunication does occur, have your reaction planned in advance. That way you won't look quite so ridiculous should you find yourself in your own "sticky" situation!

Heavenly Father,
Thank You for the opportunity to laugh. Help me to find joy in everything that I do. Let me laugh and be cheerful, so that those around me will be blessed by my smile and my optimism. Amen.

Date Night

Let your fountain be blessed,
And rejoice with the wife of your youth.

PROVERBS 5:18

My favorite getaway with Gary is a weekend at an old brownstone in New York City. Because we travel so much, we usually have enough frequent flier miles to cover our airfares. Staying at the brownstone is inexpensive, and we try to do as much free stuff as possible. We walk around Central Park, visit the Plaza Hotel, go to FAO Schwartz and window shop on Fifth Avenue. The only part of our weekend that costs much is when we eat ourselves silly in Little Italy. I've never tasted anything as delicious as the pasta and pastries in this very colorful part of New York!

I encourage you to find time to pamper your marriage. As couples, we need to find those special moments when we can gaze into each other's eyes and feel the romance of courtship again. There's nothing like dirty diapers, dirty laundry and a dirty house to put a damper on your love life. Each couple needs to find those special moments, places or occasions that put us in mind of the beauty and sacredness of the marriage relationship.

For many couples, it may be a weekend away from the kids at a bed-and-breakfast in the country. For others, it may be a picnic in the park. Perhaps your marriage could benefit from a special marriage retreat with a structured program.

Explore your options. Spending time with your spouse doesn't have to be an extravagant event. It can be as simple as my sister's idea of having a snack for two on a quilt on the bedroom floor. With the added touches of a rose, some special food treats and candle-light, this after-the-kids-are-in-bed time can be a romantic rendezvous.

I like this type of alternative to a structured "date night." After a long day chasing a three-year-old, the last thing I want to do is get dressed to go out. So Gary and I stay home while Little Gary gets to go out with his favorite babysitter, his cousin Darla. It might be to McDonald's or a pizza place or the pet shop. Whatever they want to do is fine. That way, Gary and I have some time alone as a couple, Little Gary gets to go to one of his favorite places—and I don't even have to put on heels!

The most important thing a mother can do for her children is to love their father.

Unknown

Heavenly Father,
Thank You for the mate that You've given to me. Help me to treat him as lovingly as I did in the first days of our relationship. And may he see me as the woman that he fell in love with, full of hope at the prospect of our lives together. Let our love for each other be evident to those around us, especially our children. Amen

Old Mr. Hoover

*But the Fruit of the Spirit is love, joy, peace, longsuffering,
kindness, goodness, faithfulness, gentleness, self-control.
Against such there is no law.*

GALATIANS 5:22-23

O K, so the subjects of this story (whose names
have been changed) weren't exactly walking in
the Spirit on this particular day. The stresses
of work, extracurricular school activities and family life
in general had taken their toll on Sam and Sue. They had
been going ninety miles per hour for several weeks, and
everything came to a head one evening.

Sam and Sue had been "discussing" some of their frustrations as Sue frantically tried to get some house-work
done before the family left to attend yet another function.
As she vacuumed the carpet, she and Sam continued to
bicker. Sam, feeling as if he was making no progress in the
conversation, and not knowing what to do to calm Sue's
frustrations, disappeared into the bed-room to make a
telephone call.

He called his mother-in-law to see if she had any advice on how to handle his wife, her daughter. His mother-
in-law said, "You two have been under a lot of stress, and
you've been burning the candle at both ends for too long
now. You need to slow down and get some rest. Once this
frenzied pace is stopped, things will be back to normal."

As Sam was listening to his mother-in-law's advice,
the bedroom door swung open. Sue, who was coming
into the bedroom to continue her vacuuming, had heard
a part of Sam's telephone conversation and immediately
knew to whom he was talking, and why. Furious with Sam
for calling her mother, she picked up the Hoover canister

vacuum she was using and hoisted it through the air, right at Sam!

I don't know how, but *somehow*, Sue's action broke the tension of the last few weeks, and Sam and Sue had a big laugh over the whole incident. In relating this story to a friend, Sam said, 'Boy, you haven't lived until you've seen 'Old Mr. Hoover' flying through the air at you!"

Maybe it's because the whole situation was so ridiculous, but the "Mr. Hoover" incident has become a memorable piece of Sam and Sue's family history. Every time the story is mentioned, everyone laughs hysterically.

The moral of this story is not to pick up the nearest appliance and throw it at your mate when you are angry. No, what this family learned is to not allow the pressures of trying to "do it all" bring friction into the home. They have cut back on outside activities. Sam resigned from a couple of committees, and Sue has stopped volunteering for *every* job at the kids' school. They have found that these changes have greatly relieved the stresses they were experiencing at home.

Last time I heard about them, Sue was exhibiting more self-control, but Sam is still a little skittish around vacuum cleaners!

> *The true test of walking in the spirit will not only be the way we <u>act</u>, but the way we <u>react</u> to the daily frustrations of life.*

Beverly LaHaye

Heavenly Father,

Help me to become more godly as I discipline my outward behaviors and my inward feelings. Forgive when I fail to walk in the Spirit, and may I exhibit the fruit of Your Spirit in everything that I do. Amen.

Not Too Far From Here

Somebody's down to their last dime
Somebody's running out of time
Not too far from here
Somebody's got nowhere else to go
Somebody needs a little hope
Not too far from here

And I may not know their name
But I'm praying just the same
That you'll use me Lord, to wipe away a tear
'Cause somebody's crying
Not too far from here

Somebody's troubled and confused
Somebody's got nothing left to lose
Not too far from here
Somebody's forgotten how to trust
Somebody's dying for love
Not to far from here

It may be a stranger's face
But I'm praying for your grace
To move in me and take away the fear
'Cause somebody's hurting
Not to far from here

Help me, Lord, not to turn away from pain
Help me not to rest while those around me weep
Give me your strength and compassion
When somebody finds the road of life too steep

Now I'm letting down my guard
And I'm opening my heart
Help me speak your love to every needful ear
Jesus is waiting not too far from here
Oh, Jesus is waiting
Not too far from here

Not Too Far From Here

But may the God of all grace, who called us to His eternal glory by Christ Jesus, after you have suffered a while, perfect, establish, strengthen, and settle you.

1 PETER 5:10

*I*n early 1985, I received an invitation to be on the "700 Club" telethon. When I arrived at the television studio, I was informed that I would be used that evening as a telephone counselor to take pledges from supporters and to pray with people who called for salvation or any special needs.

That night I received a phone call from a young woman that changed my life.

Susan was seventeen years old, and she was a prostitute, a drug addict and an alcoholic. To top it all off, she had just found out that she was pregnant.

It was the last straw, she said. What would she do with a baby? Susan confided that she couldn't kill a baby by having an abortion, so she had decided to kill herself.

Can you imagine my horror? This is my first night to be a counselor of any type, and I get *this* call. What do I do? I started flipping frantically through my "counselor's handbook," but I soon realized it wasn't going to help. As Susan continued talking, I silently prayed for the Lord's guidance in speaking to this desperate young woman.

To make a long story short, Susan accepted Jesus as her Savior that night. I gave her my telephone number, and she gave me hers, so that we could stay in contact,

Over the next ten years, Susan and I had many heart-to-heart conversations. We talked about God loving her no matter what. We discussed the consequences of her actions before becoming a Christian. We cried when she miscarried. She had no close family relationships, so she spent two Christmas holidays with my family. Susan visited Gary and me in Nashville. In short, I tried to be there for her.

Susan brought a new dimension into my life. I had never before known anyone who had been a prostitute or a drug addict. Through my relationship with this precious girl, I found out that my own sins were no less sinful than hers; they were just better hidden.

As time went on, Susan and I stayed in touch with each other, but gradually the time between phone calls grew farther and farther apart. Weeks stretched into months. I knew I should call to see how she was doing, but I just kept putting it off. Then two years ago, on my birthday, the phone rang. It was my dad.

"Kim," he said, and I knew by the tone of his voice that something was wrong. "We just got a call from a friend of Susan's. She said Susan had been sick, and had been hospitalized for the past two weeks. I hesitated to call you on your birthday, but I thought you would want to know ... Susan died today."

My heart sank. Why hadn't I tried to get in touch with her? I was glad that Susan had had the foresight to tell her friends to contact me. Otherwise, I may not have ever known what had happened. My consolation in the matter was, of course, knowing that Susan was no longer sick or lonely. Now she's singing with the angels in heaven.

Susan taught me many things over the course of our ten-year friendship. Her final lesson, though, was perhaps the most important: Don't put off doing something that you feel led to do. We always think that we can do a good deed or say a kind word or give attention to a special need tomorrow. Sometimes there is no tomorrow, only today.

Heavenly Father,

Teach me not to procrastinate but to do what I can today,
because there is no promise for tomorrow. Lead me to
those people who are in need of something that I can give.
I want to be available for You to use in any way that You
should choose. Amen.

Homeless in Beverly Hills

And the King will answer and say to them, "Assuredly, I say to you, inasmuch as you did it to one of the least of these My brethren, you did it to Me."

MATTHEW 25:40

Gary and I have a dear friend, Gregg, who travels with us on our concert tours as road manager and sound engineer. Gregg's parents live in Beverly Hills, California. So on one of our California tours, we decided to "tough it out" and spend the night at Gregg's parents' home.

Shortly after we got to town, it was time for dinner, so we decided on the most kid-friendly restaurant in Beverly Hills, which also happens to be my favorite place: a rib joint called R.J.'s. One of the reasons I love R.J.'s is it has a salad bar that's about a mile long. And since I had just found out that I was pregnant, this abundance of food sounded like a dream come true.

That night we ate until we were almost sick but couldn't leave until we had ordered the dessert specialty, a seven-layer chocolate cake almost a foot high. Even with eight of us at dinner, we couldn't eat the whole cake, so the waiter elegantly wrapped it in gold foil in the shape of a swan. Little Gary was fascinated with the swan and carried it proudly out of the restaurant.

We were walking next door to the parking lot on a beautiful California night when an older black man walked up to me and asked if I had any leftovers that he could have. I was momentarily shocked. This is Beverly Hills, one of the richest cities in the world. I never imagined that there might be anyone hungry or homeless here.

I gained my composure and said, "Little Gary, give this man your cake."

Little Gary lifted up his precious gold swan and offered it to the man, who said, "Oh, no, I can't take this young man's cake."

I assured him that my son had had plenty of cake already, and that he was welcome to take it. Just then, this homeless man looked at me and asked, "Do you sing gospel music?"

"Yes, sir," I answered.

"I think I've seen you singing on TV," he said.

About that time, Gary came walking over to see why I was talking to this stranger. The man said, "And I know I've seen this handsome guy singing with you. At the shelter where I stay sometimes, they allow me to watch Christian television, and I've seen you sing on my favorite program."

This man continued to tell us that many years ago he had been a pastor, but through a series of terrible circumstances he had lost his church, his family ... everything. And now, years later, he was homeless in Beverly Hills. He asked us to remember to pray for "Pastor Richard" and we have many times.

As Gary and I talked with Pastor Richard that night, I noticed that he was not drunk or high. He was just hungry, homeless and alone. What could we do? Why did it seem like praying wouldn't be enough? Should I volunteer at a homeless shelter? Serve food at a soup kitchen?

I don't have any specific answers yet, but I know that Pastor Richard has had a profound impact on my life. I've been reevaluating my "ministry" to see if I'm doing enough to minister to those in need. You sure don't have to go very far to find hurting, needy people. They're everywhere: next door, across the ocean, even in Beverly Hills. What will we do to reach them?

Heavenly Father,
Speak to me so that I will know how to reach the lost and
dying world around me. Give me the words to say when
I have an opportunity to speak to someone in need. May
my eyes see those around me as You see them, and may
my heart be filled with Your compassion to reach them.
Amen.

The Ministry of Compassion

*And He said to them, "Go into all the world and preach
the gospel to every creature."*

<blockquote>
MARK 16:15
</blockquote>

On the refrigerator at home, there is a picture
Diandra, an eight-year-old girl from Peru
whom my family sponsors through Compas-
sion International. Gary and I have been involved with
Compassion International for over seven years now, and
we have been greatly impressed with their organization.

I've traveled to Ecuador and Brazil to see the work of
Compassion in the field. Sponsored children receive food,
clothing, medical attention and an education. The most
important ministry of Compassion, though, is the teaching of Christianity to the children. Most children in the
Compassion program become Christians, and many of
their family members do as well.

We have sponsored three children in these past seven
years. Gary and I have been blessed by the letters we've
received from our sponsored children, telling of their lives
and expressing their appreciation for our support.

Recently, though, the picture of Diandra on our refrigerator has been the topic of much conversation in our
house. Little Gary noticed the picture one day, and he
asked who was in the photo. I explained to him that her
name is Diandra and that she is a girl we send money to so
that she can have food to eat, go to school and hear about
Jesus. My son's eyes were as big as saucers as he listened
to my explanation. He said, 'she doesn't have any food?" I
tried to explain that without our help she wouldn't get to
eat as well as she does now.

Little Gary went off to play, and I didn't expect to hear about this particular subject again. But the next time he walked by the refrigerator, he was very concerned and asked, "She doesn't have any food?" So we talked about Diandra again.

Every night at devotions we ask Little Gary what he wants to pray about. He always wants to pray for Diandra. His interest over the needs of a child he has never even met is puzzling. Why should he care? The conclusion that I've come to is he cares because *we* care. We've talked compassionately about Diandra, so now our son has begun to feel sympathy for her.

The lesson Little Gary is learning about caring for those in need is an important one. I used to wonder how those of us who were not missionaries spending our lives in foreign fields could "go into all the world." I've come to realize how: we do it through organizations such as Compassion International. They are able to reach out to millions of needy people all over the world, but without our help it would be an impossible task.

Mother Teresa once said, "We can do no great things—only small things with great love." She spent her life in poverty in India, living out that message by reaching out to and sharing the gospel with the poorest of the poor. Supporting organizations that minister to the most downtrodden is our way of doing small things with great love. And in the process, we teach our children valuable lessons about our responsibilities as Christians to those less fortunate.

Heavenly Father,
Speak to me today concerning how to reach out to the
world. From the youngest to the oldest, there is something
we all can do. Allow me to set an example of compassion
and concern for others to my children. Amen.

I Call Her Blessed

Her children rise up and call her blessed;
Her husband also, and he praises her:
"Many daughters have done well,
But you excel them all."
Charm is deceitful and beauty is vain,
But a woman who fears the Lord,
She shall be praised.

PROVERBS 31:28-30

My grandmother, Mary Boyce, recently celebrated her eighty-ninth birthday. She was married to my "Pop" for sixty-two years until his death in 1993. She had two children, three grandchildren—and six great-grandchildren, with another one on the way!

Gramma has lived in every decade of the twentieth century. She saw the Roaring Twenties, delivered my dad on the night that FDR was elected to his first presidential term, struggled through the Great Depression and participated in air raid blackouts during World War II. She still walks every day, plays the piano beautifully and practices the lost art of letter writing.

In recent years, I've had the opportunity to re-read some of her old letters. In the process, I have rediscovered the strength of character she possesses as well as her unwavering love and commitment for her family. Those qualities got her through many difficult times, including eighteen years of her life that she spent loving and caring for her invalid daughter, Betty Ruth.

My dad was ten years old when Betty Ruth was born. She was a beautiful baby with big brown eyes. For the first three months of her life Betty Ruth appeared to be fine.

But when her daughter was four months old, Gramma noticed something was wrong. Betty Ruth's eyes were not focusing properly and she didn't visually follow moving objects that were put in front of her.

After repeated doctor visits, the devastating prognosis was made: irreversible, permanent brain damage. This explanation of Betty Ruth's condition was in no way complete or satisfactory, but in 1942 it was all the information my grandparents received.

Betty Ruth was an invalid her entire life. Although she lived to be eighteen, she only grew to be the size of a six-year-old. Her limbs were twisted. She had epileptic-type seizures. She never spoke a word.

Gramma changed and washed diapers every day for eighteen years. She spoon-fed Betty Ruth every bite the girl ate for eighteen years. She walked the floors with her daughter in a stroller every night for eighteen years so that Pop could sleep.

The most amazing thing about my grandmother is that she never complained. I've often wondered how she made it for all those years, caring for an invalid child twenty-four hours a day. Her only relief was when Pop or her father would watch Betty Ruth so that Gramma could play the organ at church on Sundays. Her strong faith in God and her love of her family sustained her. I call her blessed.

If you are in need of love, hope or encouragement today, my prayer is that my grandmother's story will be a source of inspiration to you. Perhaps if you have a little extra time or energy available, you will reach out to someone who needs to know that at least two people care about their needs: you and Jesus.

Heavenly Father,
Thank You for the encouragement of another woman's
struggle and victory down a hard road of life. May her
example of faithfulness and love sink into my heart.
Remind me of my blessings even when I'm walking through
a valley of tears and sorrows, and help me to reach out to
others in need with the hope that You give. Amen.

The Wise Man Built His House
Upon The Rock

The wise man built his house upon the rock
The wise man built his house upon the rock
The wise man built his house upon the rock
And the rains came tumbling down

The rains came down and the floods came up
The rains came down and the floods came up
The rains came down and the floods came up
And the house on the rock stood firm

The foolish man built his house upon the sand
The foolish man built his house upon the sand
The foolish man built his house upon the sand
And the rains came tumbling down

The rains came down and the floods came up
The rains came down and the floods came up
The rains came down and the floods came up
And the house on the sand went SPLAT!

So build your house on the Lord Jesus Christ
So build your house on the Lord Jesus Christ
So build your house on the Lord Jesus Christ
And the blessings will come down

The blessings will come down as the prayers go up
The blessings will come down as the prayers go up
The blessings will come down as the prayers go up
So build your house on the Lord!

The Wise Man Built His House
Upon the Rock

*And these words which I command you today shall be
in your heart; you shall teach them diligently to your
children, and shall talk of them when you sit in your house,
when you walk by the way, when you lie down, and when
you rise up.*

DEUTERONOMY 6:6-7

My favorite part of the day has become the
time Gary and I spend having devotions
with Little Gary in his bed at night. This
time is very special: not only are we all cuddled in bed
together, but my son is learning Bible stories and songs
right before our eyes. It's amazing to me how quickly his
mind absorbs, and then retains, the things he's learning
every night.

Gary loves to say that he was born and raised in
church. "Well, we had a house," he says, "but we were in
church a lot!" I had the same experience growing up, so
we knew that being in church would be a large part of our
family life. And yet the importance of a family devotional
time has taken on a new significance as we see the results
in Little Gary's life.

I came across a topical note in my Bible that has been
encouraging to me. It says:

A Christ-centered home offers unlimited poten-
tial to study the Bible, to learn theology through
object lessons built into the structure of the home,
and to give a "word about God" to the world
through the testimony of the lives and interac-

tions of family members. Incarnational living, in which parents make it possible for their children to see the sanctification process in their own lives, is crucial.

In other words, the parents live it, and the children learn it. At this stage, creativity in teaching spiritual principles, Scripture verses and Bible stories is crucial. I can't read the King James Version of a Bible story in a monotone to my three-year-old. I have to find things that capture his attention, like reading stories from a children's devotional book or Bible with so much enthusiasm that he thinks this is the most exciting story *I've* ever heard!

It's fun to talk about bugs, leaves, trees and lions, and to let my son know that God made them all. And singing songs and listening to children's music tapes are two of our favorite ways of learning about the Lord. Little Gary's favorite song is "The Wise Man Built His House upon the Rock." This song is a "hit" with him because there are hand motions and a big SPLAT. Whatever the reason, though, the principle behind the song is getting through.

If you are not having devotions with your children, let me encourage you to do so. If you have already started a family devotional time, keep it up. The rewards are immeasurable—those blessings really do keep coming down!

Heavenly Father,
Constantly remind me of the responsibility I have to teach my children about You. Help me find ways throughout the day to tell them of Your love, mercy and majesty. Amen.

This Too Shall Pass

Whereas you do not know what will happen tomorrow. For what is your life? It's even a vapor that appears for a little time and then vanishes away.

JAMES 4:14

While we were visiting my in-laws, Gary came in to show me a poster. It was a picture of my husband at the age of nine in his hockey uniform. He was on the ice, hockey stick in hand, looking very serious about the game. Of course, I thought he was the cutest little guy ever, but as I was looking at his face, I became melancholy. I'm sure to Gary's parents it didn't seem like too long ago that their son was this little boy in the poster. Now he's a grown man with a family of his own.

Since becoming a mother, I've become a reformed "future thinker." That means I used to constantly plan for the future, but now I live for today. The lyrics to the old song have taken on new meaning for me:

> We have this moment to hold in our hands
> And to touch as it slips through our fingers like sand
> Yesterday's gone and tomorrow may never come
> But we have this moment today.

My todays are different than they used to be. I used to be occupied with planning business opportunities, traveling constantly and doing a tremendous amount of office work. Now these types of activities have greatly decreased, and most of my time is spent chasing after a very active three-year-old boy.

And you know what? 1 wouldn't have it any other way! Career fulfillment is OK, and I enjoyed that phase of my life. But I'm much happier now. You see, now when I crawl out of bed in the morning, it's not to get ready for work ... but because a little blond cutie is standing beside my bed, patting me on the head, wanting someone to play with him. To me, that's a whole lot more rewarding than anything I ever accomplished as a career woman.

I'm certainly not saying that no woman should have a career. Some people work out of financial necessity or for various other reasons. But I personally have found more fulfillment in being a hands-on mom than in any other career.

Time is so short. Children grow and change so quickly. I don't want to miss one part of the process.

Two of my son's colorful "masterpieces" are tacked up on the wall in our garage, where we can see his finger paintings every time we walk up or down the stairs. My favorite part of Little Gary's artwork, though, is the spot where you can see one little handprint, all by itself. That same hand is bigger now, and I'm glad that I've been there for all of the moments that have taken place in between.

*A baby enters your home
and makes so much noise for twenty years
you can hardly stand it—
then departs, leaving the house so silent
you think you'll go mad.*

Dr. J.A. Holmes

Heavenly Father
Thank You for the privilege of having children. Allow
every day that I'm blessed to be a mother to be a special
experience. Help me to savor ever moment that comes,
and may my children always be confident in my love and
devotion to them. Amen.

Grass Soup

For He established a testimony in Jacob,
And appointed a law in Israel,
Which He commanded our fathers,
That they should make them known to their children;
That the generation to come might know them,
The children who would be born,
That they may arise and declare them to their children,
That they may set their hope in God,
And not forget the works of God,
But keep His commandments.

PSALM 78:5-7

Gary and I recently had dinner with one of our favorite couples, Jeff and Carmen. We ate at a terrific Italian restaurant with a beautiful, quiet atmosphere. And yet when we were given the opportunity to completely relax and enjoy some stimulating adult conversation, guess what we talked about? Our kids, of course! I don't think that we lack for other subject material, but we just enjoy telling stories about our children, so we find ourselves doing it often.

During the course of the conversation that evening, we were discussing the importance of teaching our children spiritual principles and the challenges we sometimes face in doing so. Jeff told the story of a conversation he had had with his four-year-old daughter, Brette.

One day Brette was outside playing and Jeff decided to sit down and spend some time with her. After talking about the usual subjects that four-year-olds are interested in, the conversation turned to Jesus, heaven and how

Brette could ask Jesus into her heart and one day live with Jesus in heaven.

Jeff told us that he thought, "This is it. My daughter is comprehending the idea of salvation and of asking Jesus to be her Savior."

He compassionately asked his precious daughter, "Brette, would you like to know how to ask Jesus into your heart?"

She thoughtfully looked at her daddy and said, "Well, right now I have to go make some grass soup, but I'll get back to you on it!'

Needless to say, Jeff sat stunned as Brette ran off to prepare her favorite delicacy. The "moment" that he thought that they were having was just a memory now. Brette will most likely never remember the specifics of this particular father-daughter chat, but it will be one of the many building blocks that will eventually lay the foundation for her understanding of Christian theology and principles.

How many times do we as parents feel as if we're trying to teach fidgety, uninterested little creatures who will never "get it?" Let's not despair; we're on a great mission. We are, slowly but surely, teaching our children through word and example how to keep His commandments.

Heavenly Father,
Thank You for the opportunity of teaching my children
about You. May I be aware of ways to instill Your truth
in play- times, conversations and devotions with my little
ones. Let the example that I set reflect Your image. Amen.

A Smart Mouth

Everyone should be quick to listen, slow to speak and slow to become angry, for man's anger does not bring about the righteous life that God desires.

JAMES 1:19-20, NIV

I am the oldest of the three daughters in my family. As is the case with many firstborn children, I was an independent, headstrong entertainer from the day I came home from the hospital. My parents have many adorable stories of the cute things I would say and do, including dancing on the coffee table for the merriment of relatives.

Somewhere along the way, though—I think it was during my teen years—all those cute things I would say turned into something completely different. I developed what my mother called a "smart mouth."

Where I come from, having a 'smart mouth" is most definitely *not* a compliment. Learning to control my tongue has been a major issue in my life. One of the greatest compliments I can imagine is when my friends (especially my husband!) tell me that they can't believe I ever had to deal with this character problem. What a great testimony of God's ability to change someone!

Studying the Book of Proverbs, especially chapter ten, I've learned that "you are what you say." Here is one of my favorites:

The mouth of the righteous brings forth wisdom.

PROVERBS 10:31

Think about it. If the mouth of the *righteous* brings forth wisdom, what does this say about those who utter words that are foolish, harsh, deceptive, slanderous or dishonorable? Those attempting to become wise and righteous must carefully guard their words.

This principle becomes especially important to follow when there are children around. They believe what we say. They take our words to heart, whether good, bad or ugly. And nothing robs a child of his dignity faster than harsh, humiliating, belittling words spoken by a parent. We must be certain that our words are sensitive, caring and loving, especially when we speak them to the very sensitive and vulnerable children God has placed in our care.

Heavenly Father,
May the words I speak today be edifying, comforting and loving. Even in time of discipline, help my voice to resonate with Your care. Amen.

A Man of God

*Brethren, join in following my example, and note those
who so walk, as you have us for a pattern.*

PHILIPPIANS 3:17

When my first album came out, I was asked to tour with Michael W. Smith and his band. During part of the tour, we were invited to spend a couple of our days off between concerts at the Billy Graham Evangelist headquarters at Montreat, North Carolina. Not only was it an honor to be a guest of this wonderful ministry, but we were housed in the beautiful old home where Billy and Ruth Graham had raised their children.

During our stay, I needed to make some phone calls for business. But since the home where we were staying was not lived in regularly, there was no phone in the house. I walked next door to the ministry headquarters to see if there was a telephone that I could use. The receptionist listened to my request and said, "Of course. Go right down this hall, and you can use the telephone in the first office on the right."

I thanked her for her help and proceeded to walk the twenty or so feet down the hall and through the open door of the first office on the right. I was immediately surprised by the size of the office. It was huge! For a moment I wondered whose office this was. Beautifully furnished, the room contained many framed photos of Billy Graham with presidents, dignitaries and world leaders. There were also plaques on the walls, which had been given to Mr. Graham in honor of his many accomplishments. Then it hit me ... this was Billy Graham's office!

I turned around quickly, hoping no one had noticed that I had stupidly walked into the wrong office and ended up someplace where I most certainly didn't belong. I went back immediately to the receptionist's desk.

"I'm sorry," I said, "but I seem to have made a mistake. Did you say I should use the telephone in the first office to the *right*?"

"Yes, that's correct," she said cheerily.

"But that looks like Mr. Graham's office," I replied.

"It is," she said. "He's not coming in today, and I'm sure he wouldn't mind your using his telephone."

With a stunned look on my face, I managed to say, "Oh, OK."

I walked very slowly down the hallway this time, and I tried to act as if this sort of thing happened to me everyday. As I turned and walked through the door, I very reverently made my way over to the desk where the telephone sat. Now, who was I supposed to call? In the excitement of the past few moments, I couldn't remember. But I knew that I had better call someone.

I slowly dialed my parents' telephone number as I once again looked around at the things in the office. This was unbelievable. When my parents were both on the phone, I told them where I was. Needless to say, they couldn't believe it either.

Some of you may be reading this story and thinking, "So what?" But I'll bet that most of you can relate to the feeling of awe that I experienced that day.

Why? Because Billy Graham is probably the most respected Christian leader of this century. He has led millions of people to salvation in Jesus Christ through his evangelistic crusades and television ministry. He has counseled and prayed with every president since Harry S. Truman. He appears on secular television shows and always says exactly the right thing at the right time. In short, Billy Graham has lived the life that he has preached about for the past fifty years.

I'm not saying that Mr. Graham is perfect. No, he's human. But he has certainly lived a life that serves as an example to us all. In an age of searching for heroes for ourselves and our children, here's one man who can be wholeheartedly endorsed as a role model.

As I sat in Mr. Graham's chair at his desk, using his telephone that day, I was well aware of the atmosphere of holiness that permeated his office. How many great decisions that had affected the world for Jesus had been made from this place? I would probably never know the answer to that question. But I do know I was hoping that some of the greatness I felt in that office would somehow rub off on me.

When we see great men and women, we give credit to their mothers.

Charlotte Perkins Gilman

Heavenly Father,
Thank You for role models that I can look to as a source of inspiration and guidance. You are the ultimate in perfection. Help me to strive to be more like You. Amen.

My Sweetie Pie

He's my little sweetie, sweetie pie
He's my little sweetie, sweetie, sweetie guy
And when it comes to sweetie pies, none compare
To the precious boy with the kooky hair.

My Sweetie Pie

But Jesus said, "Let the little children come to Me, and do not forbid them; for of such is the kingdom of heaven."

MATTHEW 19:14

Perhaps the saddest commentary I've heard on loving children came from my own great-grandfather. He and my great-grandmother had a beautiful baby boy. They loved him dearly, but he died at the age of eighteen months. Some superstitious person in rural Alabama in the early 1900s told my great-grandparents that the Lord took the baby because they loved him too much. And unfortunately, this guilt-producing theory was believed. I've often wondered how this experience affected the other six children in the family.

Children are made to be loved. How is it possible to love them too much? I suppose that if we begin to idolize children, a problem might arise. Most parents, though, do not run the risk of thinking of their children as little gods and goddesses. We are usually well aware our children's faults, but we love them in spite of their shortcomings. An unknown author once wrote:

> *I do not love him because he is good,*
> *but because he is my little child.*

Perhaps a form of loving children too much could manifest itself in over protectiveness. I read of a woman who was so paranoid of something terrible happening to her children that she was unable to do anything except watch them all day long as they played. She didn't cook any meals, clean her house or accomplish anything because she was so fearful of harm coming to her children.

The poor woman needed psychological help to overcome this powerful obsession.

I love my son wholeheartedly. In fact, as I write this I'm at the place many first-time mothers find themselves ... pregnant again, and wondering whether the love I have for my first child will stretch far enough for a second baby. Every mother I've spoken to, though, assures me that somehow the love that is felt for the first child is multiplied beyond what can be imagined as each new child comes along.

It's in the daily living of life and raising of children that we express our love to them most effectively. When we unselfishly give of ourselves in order to meet the needs of the little ones entrusted to our care, true love is shown.

From the time of my son's birth, I have been singing a silly song to him. Now that he is three years old, he loves singing "My Sweetie Pie" along with me to the tune of "I'm a Little Teapot." It's a frivolous little song, but my son thinks it is very special because it's about him. He knows when I sing it to him, what I'm really saying is, "I love you."

Heavenly Father,
Help me today to express love to my children. May they know, even when being disciplined, that I love them completely and unconditionally. Fill my heart with gratitude and appreciation at the privilege of being a mother. Amen.

The Jerk at Walt Disney World

And now a word to you parents. Don't keep on scolding
and nagging your children, making them angry and
resentful. Rather, bring them up with the loving discipline
the Lord himself approves, with suggestions and godly
advice.

EPHESIANS 6:4, TLB

*G*ary, Little Gary and I recently spent a day at
Disney World with Gary's sister Maralee and
her family. I was waiting to see what ride we
would go on next when I spotted a grown man carelessly
pulling an adorable six-year-old blonde girl by the arm.
As he passed by, I heard him say to her, 'You stupid little
crybaby. I've had just about enough of you!"

Needless to say, I was outraged. My first reaction was
to jump up and intervene. But the man and little girl were
quickly lost in the crowd, so I could only angrily report
the incident to my family.

I had calmed down a bit when we arrived at our desti-
nation for the next ride. And guess who was right in front
of us. The same guy! I immediately told my family that
this was 'the jerk." (I don't usually make it a practice to
call someone by that name, but this person deserved the
title.)

I spent the remainder of our time in line staring at
him, looking for any indication that he would erupt at the
child again. I knew that if it were to happen again, I would
not keep quiet. Then he would probably yell at me, Gary
would have to defend me, there would be an ugly scene,
possibly a fight, and we would be escorted out of the front
gates of the Magic Kingdom.

In his book *The Strong-Willed Child*, Dr. James Dobson writes:

> *The spirit of a child is a million times more vulnerable than his will. It is a delicate flower that can be crushed and broken all too easily (and even unintentionally). The spirit relates to the self-esteem or personal worth that a child feels. It is the most fragile characteristic in human nature, being particularly vulnerable to rejection and ridicule and failure.*

Imagine the damage done to the little blonde girl's spirit by the cruel words of the person I assumed was her father. And if he demeaned her in public, imagine what happens at home! I've heard my dad say that the words a parent uses to describe his child will determine what the child becomes. Why? Because a child believes and takes to heart what a parent says.

What will our children become because of the words we use to describe them? Stupid crybabies or precious, intelligent, loved blessings? The choice is ours.

Heavenly Father,
Please give me the patience of Job, the wisdom of Solomon and the love of Jesus as I deal with my children. Help me to remain in control of my emotions as I attempt to teach my children to gain control of their emotions. Remind me daily that children are a blessing and let me always be thankful for the privilege of being a parent. Amen.

You're the Boss

The rod and reproof give wisdom,
But a child left to himself brings shame to his mother.

PROVERBS 29:15

Gary and I are teaching our son to say words that kind and good. We are also teaching Little Gary which types of words he is *not* allowed to say, carefully weeding phrases like 'shut up" and "leave me alone" from his growing vocabulary.

Along with the "language lessons," we are also teaching our son about obedience and who is in charge. I know he understands what we are saying, because he answers correctly every time we ask him, "Who's the boss?" But understanding and obeying don't necessarily go hand in hand.

Last week, Gary was reprimanding Little Gary for playing with the gum he was chewing. He said, "If you touch it once more, I'll take the gum away from you."

Testing his limits, Little Gary murmured softly, "No, you won't."

Gary looked him squarely in the eye and said, "What did you say, young man?"

Realizing his mistake, Little Gary quickly changed his approach. "You're the boss!" he sweetly replied.

These are the types of confrontations parents deal with daily when young children are trying to see "who's the boss." Even when they know, they will still test the boundaries. One of our many parental responsibilities is to set and guard the boundaries consistently.

We as parents have a limited amount of time in which to teach and discipline our children. If we start disciplining early, the amount of chastisement necessary will diminish as the child gets older. So the opposite would also be true. If we don't begin disciplining early in a child's life, it will become harder as the years go by. Since we are training our children to ultimately obey God as *the* authority figure in their lives, our responsibility to discipline is one we should take very seriously. Because He is, as Little Gary says, "the *REALLY* Big Boss."

Heavenly Father,
Teach me how to properly and fairly discipline my
children, so that I may bring them to an understanding
of Your authority in their lives. As they grow older, may
the guidelines and principles I have taught them lead
them to a life of self-control based on following Your
commandments. Amen.

A Time to Laugh

To everything there is a season,
A time for every purpose under heaven...
A time to weep,
and a time to laugh.

ECCLESIASTES 3:1, 4A

*L*ittle Gary and I were having lunch at a fast-food restaurant with some of Gary's relatives who were in town. As we were finishing up our meal, Little Gary reached over and helped himself to his cousin Anna's last Chicken Nugget. He started eating it before I could stop him. I said, "Gary, do not reach over and take Anna's food!"

Anna said, "That's OK, I was finished anyway."

I continued to Gary, "If you want something to eat from someone else's plate, you need to ask if it's all right for you to have the food."

My son innocently looked at me and shook his head. "I *can't* talk with my mouth full!"

What could I say? He was right. He had been told time and again not to talk with his mouth full. I had no timely comeback, and trying to explain that I meant to ask *before* he put the food in his mouth was lost in the laughter of the relatives at the table.

I'm amazed at the quickness of my son's mind and the intelligence he is displaying at the ripe old age of three. I'm already worried that by the time he's seven or eight, he'll be able to reason beyond my ability to keep up with him.

Everyone has stories about the cute, funny, absurd and intelligent things their children say. I was at my parents' home recently and was looking through the baby book in which my grandmother had written faithfully for the first few years of my dad's life. There was one story about the time she had found my dad's teddy bear with its head missing. She decided to put the bear into the clothes hamper and then eventually throw the bear out without my dad's knowledge.

Well, Dad found the teddy bear in the hamper and questioned my grandmother as to why he was in there. Gramma explained that she had put the bear in the hamper to "rest" and that the bear hadn't said anything about not liking being in there. Dad looked at her and said, "Well, he couldn't say anything without his head!"

I have never laughed as much as I have since my son began talking. And how angry can we get at a child who says things that make us chuckle? The guileless innocence of a child's assessment of a situation can put our own hardened attitudes into perspective. One of the great joys of motherhood is the happiness our children bring into our lives. Let's make the effort to experience the laughter of childhood with our children.

Heavenly Father,
Thank You for this season of my life when I have children
around to make me laugh. May I always find joy in the
words and actions of my children. Allow me to experience
the happiness of being young and carefree with my little
ones. Amen.

Learn to Live With It

Which of you by worrying can add one cubit to his stature?
MATTHEW 6:27

My nieces, Megan and Mandy, had spent the night with my aunt and uncle, Grace and C.T. The girls had been taken to McDonald's for breakfast and were anxious to get back to the house so they could swim in the pool. On the way home, Grace stopped by the store to pick up some chrysanthemums for the flower boxes around the pool. Impatiently, the girls waited in the car with C.T. while Grace went in to buy the flowers.

When she returned empty-handed a few minutes later, the girls thought they were on their way to the pool. But Grace was debating about what she should do. They didn't have the color flowers she had wanted. There were some that were a different color, but she didn't know if it would work as well.

C.T., who is one of the most easygoing men on earth, said to go ahead and buy them. But Megan, who was growing impatient, thought that the alternate color would never do, so they might as well go home.

Grace decided to go back inside and buy the flowers even though they weren't exactly what she had wanted. Being all of seven years old, Megan felt compelled to make her landscaping opinions known. She began to complain how the flowers were "never going to look good." Mandy, who had patiently been listening to Megan for too long now, put the whole situation into perspective as only a four-year-old can: "Well, Megan, I guess you're just gonna have to learn to live with it!"

That's good advice for all of us. Think how much happier and more contented we would be if we could stop worrying about things beyond our control. So much of what we worry about never happens anyway. We just make ourselves miserable thinking about the stuff that might happen.

It's impossible to worry and to trust God at the same time. Whether we're fretting over finances, relationships, sickness or any of the infinite number of other subjects that concern us, the bottom line is that God is in control. Worrying will not change the outcome of any situation. In the words of Barbara Johnson:

Remember:
YOU CAN BE AS HAPPY AS YOU DECIDE TO BE.

I will *choose* to be happy. Even in the most trying of situations, I want to do as Psalm 37:7 advises: "Rest in the Lord, and wait patiently for Him." Perhaps the old hymn summarizes it best:

> *Tis so sweet to trust in Jesus*
> *Just to take Him at His Word*
> *Just to rest upon His promise*
> *Just to know thus saith the Lord*
> *Jesus, Jesus, how I trust Him*
> *How I've proved Him o'er and o'er*
> *Jesus, Jesus, precious Jesus*
> *Oh, for grace to trust Him more.*

Heavenly Father,
My prayer is that I would learn to trust You more. It's
such a comfort to know that my life is in Your hands, and
the circumstances surrounding me are in Your control.
Remind me daily that choosing to be happy is an option.
May I find my strength in your joy. Amen.

Mirror of the Heart

An ordinary flower
No one even noticed she was there
Nobody cared
Afraid she was unworthy
She retreated deep into her shame
Into her pain
She prayed for consolation
And found to her surprise
What the loving hands that made you always
    recognized

There is a beauty to last a lifetime
A beauty that blooms eternally
Let the love of Jesus shine through you like a star
Till the beauty reflected in your eyes
Is a mirror of the heart
A mirror of the heart

She'd always had attention
Like a princess in a fairy tale
She could not fail
Then one day she realized
She'd built her world around a pretty face
That fades away
She prayed for something lasting
And found it deep inside
Then suddenly discovered in her father's sight...

There is a beauty to last a lifetime
A beauty that blooms eternally
Let the love of Jesus shine through you like a star
Till the beauty reflected in your eyes
Is a mirror of the heart
A mirror of the heart.

Mirror of the Heart

Charm is deceitful and beauty is vain,
But a woman who fears the Lord, she shall he praised.

PROVERBS 31:30

*L*ast night Gary's Aunt Antonia came up to me and said, "I know you probably don't feel it now, but you look beautiful!" What a considerate thing to say to a pregnant woman. No, I certainly *don't* feel it, but it's great to know there's some truth to the old adage about the "pregnant glow."

My involvement in beauty pageants and then the contemporary Christian music industry—both of which place a high emphasis on physical appearance—have forced me to do some soul-searching. I had to determine for myself the amount of importance I would place on physical beauty. One experience I had persuaded me not to overly emphasize outer beauty but rather to concentrate my energies on developing the more permanent beauty that radiates from the inside.

While Miss Florida, I was asked by a Christian college to sing for a special chapel series entitled "Women in Ministry." Although I wasn't wearing my Miss Florida crown and banner (those were only required for official events), I was decked out in my beauty queen finest. I sang my songs and sat down, confident in the knowledge that I had done a great job. I had represented the pageant well and done my duty. I could be proud of myself.

Well, I was proud of myself for about five minutes. The speaker that morning was an elderly missionary lady. She had to have been in her eighties. As she was introduced, she shuffled to the podium in her orthopedic shoes. She was wearing a simple navy blue suit with a high, buttoned collar. Her hair was neatly coiffed in a "pentecostal bun". In short, she *looked* like a missionary.

When she began to speak, I began to shrink in my chair. She said nothing negative about me, of course (my own conscience did a fine job of that), but simply told of her forty years on the mission fields of Africa. She had gone to the Dark Continent to minister along with her husband. Twenty years after their arrival, her husband died, but she stayed on another twenty years to continue their work.

She told of the children she had taught to read, the babies she had nursed back to health and the countless souls saved. The longer this dear lady spoke, the clearer the realization became to me that she was the minister. I was just the showgirl.

My concern in preparing for the chapel service had been how I looked and what I would wear, not how I would minister to the students sitting in the pews. By the time this lady finished speaking, I was wishing I could melt right into the carpet and disappear. I knew I was wrong and was terribly embarrassed by my ridiculous attitude.

The Lord used a missionary lady to bring about a big change in my heart. From that day on, I have never taken myself quite so seriously. I'm not saying that I don't like to look nice or that I don't take care of myself, but my attitude toward physical beauty has changed tremendously.

I still like going to the salon and having my hair done, and I certainly haven't given up my fascination with make-up. But true inner beauty is the result of a relationship with Jesus Christ, a contentment with the circumstances of life and a peace that can be found only by trusting in the Lord. I have found my Bible to be the greatest inner "beauty book" ever!

Heavenly Father,
Please allow me to find a balance between the emphasis that the world places on physical beauty and Your view of my body as a temple of the Holy Spirit. May I always strive to achieve an inner beauty, which is the result of a consistent relationship with You. Amen.

Wonder Woman

Who can find a virtuous wife?
For her worth is far above rubies.

I'm a fan of Martha Stewart, the queen of all things domestic. I enjoy watching her television show, and I've learned a lot from her. In fact, I may have had the only two-year-old in the country who watches "Marfa" every night! Whether she's cooking a gourmet dish, grooming an apple tree hedge into espaliers or designing a bridal bouquet, she does everything to perfection. Sometimes, though, her effortless grace makes me feel so inadequate that I just have to say, "Enough already".

The "Wonder Woman" of the Bible—the Proverbs 31 Woman—sometimes has the same effect on me. This woman is amazing. I made a partial list of this woman's accomplishments and talents and was astounded.

The Bible tells us that she rises early and works late. She would *have* to in order to accomplish everything she does. She exercises, sews, makes tapestry, buys food and cooks. In addition to her work at home, she's also a businesswoman. She makes and sells clothes, buys property and cultivates it and is prepared financially for the winter months.

She's wise, trustworthy and compassionate to the needy, certainly a woman we could strive to emulate. And yet there are two things that console me when I begin to feel that I will never measure up to this standard.

First, she has servants, and I don't. So, for those of us trying to do it all ourselves, we must prioritize and decide which things we can do and which things are not important enough to worry about. Cooking great meals for my family and becoming a wise woman are important to me; making and selling clothes and planting vineyards are not. So I'm not going to beat myself up because I don't do absolutely *everything* that this extraordinary woman does. It's the principle of being motivated, not lazy, that is the point of that chapter of Proverbs.

My second consolation is that this woman's children are grown. I've reached this conclusion because verse twenty-eight says, "Her children rise up and call her blessed." Most children do not realize that their parents are deserving of any praise until after they leave home. The Proverbs 31 Woman has already raised her children and now has more time to devote to creativity and outside interests.

Whew, that's a relief! Those of us with small children at home cannot imagine doing much of anything except the absolute necessities, especially if we work outside the home. Six weeks after Little Gary was born, I was in a recording studio, singing the vocals on a new album. I quickly had to learn how to juggle my priorities; for the first six months of Little Gary's life, it was all I could do to keep house (sort of), cook dinner, take care of a baby and attempt to look halfway presentable myself.

As I adjusted to motherhood, I slowly began to take on some of the "extras" again, such as redecorating a room, hosting a Thanksgiving celebration and even writing a book.

Then ... I got pregnant again! Oh well, I guess women have been coping with this scenario for thousands of years, and you and I will too!

Heavenly Father,
Thank You for the excellent role model of the woman in
Proverbs 31. Please allow her wonderful qualities to inspire

me to strive to be all that I can possibly be as a woman, wife and mother. May I learn to be diligent in my attempt to do "all things through Christ who strengthens me" (Philippians 4:13). Amen.

Walking in His Steps

For to this you were called, because Christ also suffered for us, leaving us an example, that you should follow His steps.

PETER 2:21

*L*ast year I read the classic *In His Steps* by Dr. Charles M. Sheldon. The book tells the story of a pastor whose life is changed by a chance encounter with a destitute man. After the man's death, the pastor challenges himself, and his congregation, to respond to every situation in life by asking the question, "What would Jesus do?"

During the last year, I have tried to consciously ask myself the question, "What would Jesus do?" I have found that the answer comes easier when dealing with big issues, such as life-changing decisions. These types of situations lend themselves to much thought and contemplation and therefore seem to merit the time and energy necessary to determine exactly what Jesus would do.

The mundane, everyday decisions, on the other hand, are harder to think of in terms of Jesus' actions. Considering what Jesus would do if, say, the toilet were clogged or the kids were out-of-sorts is a bit more difficult to do. But that is *exactly* the point! It's in the day-to-day living that our Christianity is acted out, and so that's precisely when we need to reach a decision as to what Jesus would do.

While reading *In His Steps*, I was astounded at the changes that were brought into people's lives by doing things the way Jesus would do them. The folks in the book could cut no corners on moral issues.

Businessmen could no longer be less than totally honest in their business dealings.

Rich society women could not justify their ways of life when there were starving people around them, so they gave away their fortunes to help those in need.

The pastor could not be content preaching his flowery sermons to tickle the ears of his parishioners, but was compelled to challenge them to make substantial changes in their comfortable lives.

For the characters in the book, living a truly moral life following Christ's commands required great sacrifice and it will for us, too. God has instituted the highest of moral standards, so in doing things His way, the standard must be upheld.

In his timeless devotional *My Utmost for His Highest*, Oswald Chambers wrote: "We must fight to be moral. Morality does not happen by accident; moral virtue is acquired."

As parents, perhaps our greatest responsibility is to teach our children to be morally upright. Training them to know right from wrong and good from evil is of the highest importance. We must also instill in them the desire to *want* to make the right, proper and moral decision.

This principle of morality is one that will be of benefit to a child for his entire lifetime. We must be diligent in our efforts to teach our children, as well as ourselves, to walk in His steps.

Heavenly Father,
Help me to present the highest standards of ethics in my daily life. Allow me to present to my children the moral principles that You have established in Your Word. May my example of ethical living be the pattern my children will learn to follow. Amen.

A Wise Woman

Receive my instruction, and not silver,
And knowledge rather than choice gold;
Far wisdom is better than rubies,
And all the things one may desire
cannot be compared with her.

I have this dream that someday, many years from now, I will be a grandmother sitting on the front porch, rocking in my favorite wooden rocker. Around me will be my precious little grandchildren. We will be discussing a variety of different subjects, but ultimately the conversation will turn to Jesus.

My grandchildren will ask me questions about Jesus—who He is, where He lives, how we know He's there and why He loves us so much. They may be interested in the life I have lived and want to hear stories about it as well, but my biggest hope is that they will know they can ask me questions about spiritual things and that I will be able to give them wise answers.

This type of scene will never happen if I don't live my life with the goal in mind of becoming wise. Not just being an intelligent woman, but a truly wise woman. There is an old adage that says, "If you aim at nothing, you will surely hit it." That's why I'm aiming my sights at the long-term goal of becoming wise.

So where do I start? The Scriptures say that the fear of the Lord is the beginning of knowledge (see Proverbs 1:7), so there's the starting point. But what exactly is the fear of the Lord? A terrifying dread of being thunder-struck for disobedience? No, it is a submissive reverence, an understanding of God's awesomeness which inspires us to want to become obedient servants. Once we have established the goal of obedience to God as the first priority of our lives, then we are able to search His Word to begin the journey to wisdom.

Of course, I've found there's not enough time to learn *everything* that I need to know to become a wise woman, not even on a subject as important as, say, child rearing: child psychology, proper discipline measures, health issues, how to instill spiritual foundations, safety measures and so on. So I've decided that true biblical wisdom will have to fill in the gaps where human knowledge is deficient.

Proverbs 4:7 says, "Wisdom is the principal thing; therefore get wisdom. And in all your getting, get understanding." Wisdom applies practical knowledge about God in order to live skillfully. Not only will wisdom enable skillful living, but those who fear the Lord will also acquire goodness, riches, honor and satisfaction (see Psalm 31:19), a right relationship with others (see Leviticus 25:17), mercy (see Psalm 103:17), strong confidence (see Proverbs 14:26) and God's consistent attention (see Psalm 34:7).

I've started filling journals with scriptures, quotations and devotional passages that impart wisdom. I occasionally read through what I've written in order to refresh my memory and spirit with wisdom. Perhaps a "wisdom journal" is something that you could begin keeping, too. We can begin today the journey to becoming the wise grandmas of tomorrow.

Heavenly Father,
Please honor my request to become a truly wise woman.
The desire of my heart is to put Your Word into practical use in my life. May I begin to walk the road of wisdom with You today. Amen.

The Hard Makes it Great

*All of them pleased God because of their faith! But still
they died without being given what had been promised.
This was because God had something better in store for us.
And he did not want them to reach the goal of their faith
without us.*

HEBREWS 11:39-40, CEV

*E*ver have one of those days when everything
just seems to be too hard? Getting out of bed is
an effort, saying "NO" is an ongoing task, and
picking up one more toy feels like it will put you over the
edge. This is the type of day when I need to hear about
people who have been "through the fire" and have survived.

Hebrews 11 has provided me with much-needed inspiration on the days when I feel I can't keep going. I prefer the Contemporary English Version. The great heroes
and heroines of the Bible come alive to me in this particular translation of "The Faith Chapter."

The story of Abraham and Sarah has always encouraged me. The Bible says that Abraham was "as good as
dead" when his son was born, but he became the ancestor
of many people (see Hebrews 11:12). I always feel better
about having my children in my thirties when I read this
verse; Gary and I are certainly *not as good as dead* yet!
And I guess if Abraham and Sarah found the energy in
their nineties to raise a child, I can handle mine with sixty
years less mileage on me.

This great chapter goes on to tell of Moses, Isaac, Jacob, Joseph, Rahab and others who lived extraordinary
lives of faith. It tells of people being tortured, made fun of,
beaten with whips, chained in jail, stoned to death, sawed

in two and killed with swords. Verse 38 puts my life into perspective for me every time I read it: "The world did not deserve these good people, who had to wander in deserts and on mountains and had to live in caves and holes in the ground."

Very few of us could honestly say that we have been tested like those of the saints of old were. Yet we still have our own trials and tribulations. When the circumstances of my own life seem overwhelming, I think of those who lived honorable lives in the midst of adverse situations. Then I remember the words of Jimmy Dugan in the movie *A League of Their Own*: "It's supposed to be hard. If it wasn't hard everyone would do it. It's the 'hard' that makes it great."

Heavenly Father,
Thank You for Your Word that inspires me to live each day to the fullest. Allow the lives of the heroes and heroines of the Bible to come alive in my heart and teach me to live my life for You. May my faith in You grow stronger daily. Amen.

I Fall In Love

I cry every time I take a look inside
And I'm hurting 'cause I realize what's in me
Who can know my heart and love me still?
You looked beyond it all and saw an empty life You
could fill...

Your ways never, ever fail to amaze
As the years go by such a mystery
Who can know my heart and all its shame
You love the same tomorrow, yesterday
You won't ever change

I fall in love
When I think of all You've done for me
I fall in love
It's all so much clearer now and I can see
All the memories
They bring me to my knees
I fall in love

Create in me a pure heart
Renew Your Spirit in me
Fill my mouth with praise for You
My lips will always sing

Who can know my heart and love me still
You looked beyond it all and saw an empty life
You could fill...
I fall in love.

I Fall In Love

But God demonstrates His own love toward us, in that while we were still sinners, Christ died for us.

ROMANS 5:8

I can think back over my life and remember fondly things and people that I have loved. I have always felt the love of my family, although my sisters and I have had our share of sibling rivalries. I used to love being my dad's helper. He had no sons, so as his oldest daughter, I was the one who would help him with his projects around the house.

I remember being seven years old and feeling an intense love for Jesus as I gave my heart to Him at an open-air tabernacle at youth camp. I remember the exhilaration of "puppy love" when I began to be interested in boys. And there was the love for a little blue sports car that I just *had* to have, and which is still fondly ingrained in my consciousness as a symbol of my single years.

There's the love for special friends who have been a part of my life for years and years now. I never thought I would be old enough to say, "Yeah, we've been friends for over twenty years," but I have some friends who have been with me that long and longer.

I have an enormous feeling of love for my husband Gary. I told him just the other day that after seven years of marriage, I'm still *very* pleased with my selection. And I am. I knew that I loved Gary and wanted to spend my life with him before I married him, but shortly after we were married the fact that I had made the 100 percent correct decision was confirmed to me.

We had been married a couple of months when I decided to cook steaks for dinner. Now, I had never bought or cooked a steak before in my life, so I blindly went to the store, bought some type of steak and came home and attempted to grill it in the oven. I wasn't much of a cook in those days, but I was full of enthusiasm, so I had complete confidence that this intimate, candlelight dinner would be a romantic experience.

It only took me two or three bites that night at dinner to realize that something was wrong. My steak was so tough that after attempting to swallow a couple of bites I knew this piece in my mouth was *not* going to go down. Under the pretense of getting some more water to drink, I went into the kitchen and quietly spit the chunk of meat into the garbage. As my bite of steak landed in the trash, I saw that there was already a big chunk of ABC (already been chewed) meat in the garbage. It was then that I understood why Gary had already made his own trip to the kitchen for more water. He had needed to get rid of his steak and didn't want to hurt my feelings by telling me what was wrong. Yep, I knew that I had married the perfect man for me!

Perhaps the most overwhelming feeling of love I've experienced thus far in my life occurred at the moment when my son was laid in my arms for the first time. I had the intellectual knowledge that I would love him, but until I held him, I could not possibly have comprehended the depth of the love that I would feel for him.

Still, none of the loves we feel for others can compare to the love that our Heavenly Father has for us. To think that He loved us when we didn't love Him, while we were still sinners, is an awesome thought. It is because He has loved us so immensely that we can experience love ourselves. In his book *Drawing Near*, John MacArthur wrote: "In our society, love is a common word but an uncommon experience."

Those of us who have been blessed to know the love of a family, spouse, child, friend and Savior are truly blessed indeed!

Heavenly Father,
Thank You far loving me. I'm humbled to think that You loved before I was conceived in my mother's womb, and You continue to love me today. May I always be thankful for Your love, and may I show it to those whom You have given me to love. Always remind me of the privilege of loving and being loved in return. Amen.

Megan and the Puppy

You will keep him in perfect peace, whose mind is stayed on You, because he trusts in You.

ISAIAH 26.3

My niece Megan is one of my favorite people. She's nine years old now and is growing into a wonderful young lady. Over the course of her life, she has been the source of many laughs and anecdotes. One of my favorite stories occurred when Megan was five.

Gary and I (who had no children yet) had gone to Florida for some concerts and to visit my family. When we arrived at Megan's home, she proudly showed us her new puppy. It was a tiny white puppy with blue eyes, and Megan was a great "mama" to this puppy.

While my sister Tonya, my brother-in-law Jeff, Gary and I were away from home, somehow the puppy got loose and was hit by a car. One of its back legs was broken, and we all feared the worst. Jeff decided to give the puppy until the next day to show some improvement.

Sadly, the next morning the puppy was still suffering and so, without Megan's knowledge, it just "disappeared." Later that day, Megan was told that the puppy got sick and had to go away. Although she was sad, this explanation seemed to satisfy her.

The next week when I returned home, I called my sister to chat. Before we hung up, I asked to speak to Megan. I wanted to say something comforting about the puppy situation.

"Megan," I said, "I'm really sorry about your puppy."

She was silent for a second and then said, "What puppy?"

A bit surprised I replied, "The little white puppy with the blue eyes that got sick and went away while I was at your house last week."

In true childlike fashion she said, "Oh, yeah, that one. Well, I have a new puppy now, so everything's OK."

Kids are nothing if not resilient! The adults in this scenario had anguished over how to keep the reality of what had happened to this puppy from Megan. Tonya and Jeff had worried about how this situation would affect their daughter. We had discussed how much of the story a five-year-old child would be able to understand and deal with emotionally. In short, we had tried to protect a child from the harsh realities of life and death.

I believe the right decision was made in *not* telling Megan exactly what happened to her puppy. I don't think we were dishonest. Her parents didn't feel that she was ready to deal with the whole truth at that time in her life.

This type of protection is one of our duties as parents. We are responsible for shielding our children from things and situations that could cause them harm, whether physical, emotional, mental or spiritual. How much to shelter a child and from what are daily decisions that parents must face.

These decisions should be made prayerfully and thoughtfully in order to shelter our children without over-protecting them. And we need to realize that occasionally we will make mistakes. The important thing is to be aware of our responsibility to protect the very vulnerable hearts and minds of our children.

Heavenly Father,
Please give me wisdom in daily protecting my children.
Whether it's concerning the people they come in contact
with, the television and videos they watch or the many
other issues that affect them, may I be aware of my
responsibility to guide and nurture their minds. Amen.

Forget the Housework

For the things which are seen are temporary, but the things which are not seen are eternal.

2 CORINTHIANS 4:18B

At this point in my pregnancy, my doctor has put me to bed. I had begun experiencing pre-term labor, so in order to not deliver prematurely, I've been ordered to stay off my feet. That means no shopping, no cooking, no cleaning, nothing!

I had the same condition during my first pregnancy, so I knew what to expect. The big difference this time is that I have a three-year-old son to care for. Fortunately, Gary and I work out of our home, so he is able to be "Mr. Mom" during this difficult time.

I knew from experience that the one thing that would bother me the most about being in bed for the duration of my pregnancy was not being able to keep my house. Gary is doing a great job, but like most men, if the house looks clean, then he thinks it is clean. And like most women, I know it's *not!* But in order to ensure a healthy baby, I've had to do something that's hard for me—forget the housework. As Phyllis Diller once said,

> Cleaning your house while your kids are still growing is like shoveling the walk before it stops snowing. (She's right, but I still like a tidy house.)

The other day my guys were running errands, and I was home alone. I was getting hungry (something that happens quite frequently these days), so I got up and grabbed something to eat. On my way back to the bedroom, I noticed little fingerprints on some windows and mirrors in the house. I started to get the Windex but then decided I had better not, so I made a mental note to tell Gary about them.

The next day I was reading a book and came across a quotation that brought tears to my eyes. Now, at this point I don't know if it's hormonal or if I'm being overly sentimental, but I started bawling over a line that read:

> *It will be gone before you know it.*
> *The fingerprints on the wall*
> *appear higher and higher.*
> *Then they disappear.*

Had I told Gary about the fingerprints? Had he already noticed and cleaned them? I had to know, so I went to check. They were still there: the precious little markings of a boy who is already growing up too quickly to suit his mama.

It's been a week now, and neither Gary nor I have been willing to erase the evidence. The fingerprints have become a symbol of my son's childhood and a reminder of time marching on. For the few years that I will have children in my home, I don't want housework, or anything else, to be more important than spending time with them.

The most memorable moments of my life will be spent baking cookies, playing trains and cuddling—not dusting, vacuuming and scrubbing toilets. I realize there must be a balance, but if I'm going to err, let it be in favor of my children. After they're gone, I'll have plenty of time to clean.

The darn trouble with cleaning the house
is it gets dirty the next day anyway, so skip

a week if you have to. The children are the most important thing.

Barbara Bush

Heavenly Father,
Please give the ability to see things as You see them. Help me to understand the importance of eternal things, and remind me not to focus so much energy on temporal things. May I be diligent in my home, yet more faithful to nurture the most important part of my home ... my family. Amen.

Pass It On

*For He established a testimony in Jacob, and appointed
a law in Israel, which He commanded our fathers, that
they should make them known to their children; that the
generation to come might know them, the children who
would be born, that they may arise and declare them to
their children, that they may set their hope in God, and
not forget the works of God, but keep His commandments.*

PSALM 78:5-7

A year or so before my grandfather died, I sat
down with him, my grandmother and a tape
recorder to interview them about their lives.
They told me how they met, the kind of car they drove
when they first dated, when and where they were married,
how Pop made a living, how they raised their children and
how happy they had been even through the hard times.
This tape is very special to me because it is a record of my
heritage.

It's only been within the last five years that I've begun
to take an interest in my family's history. The older I get,
the more I want to know about who I am and where I came
from. One of my most valued possessions is the antique
Victorian settee that my grandmother gave me. It's over
one hundred years old and came from her family's farm
in rural New York. I love looking at the china tea cups and
saucers that my great-grandmother hand painted when
she was a teenager. And the portrait of "Uncle John," who
was the lieutenant governor of New Hampshire in the
1700s, is especially intriguing.

I was born into a family with a long history of active
Christianity. One of my great-grandmothers played in
a Salvation Army band, another was the matriarch of a

large, Southern family that put the "church" in a Church of God. My grandmother played the organ for years at church, and my grandfather was an usher. My parents were both saved at an early age and modeled a Christian life for my sisters and me. And I married into a family with much the same heritage. Grandparents who were saved in the 1920s and 1930s, parents who were saved as children and then raised their children in the church. My son has a spiritual heritage from *both* sides of his family. That legacy is something for which to be thankful.

If you have a spiritual heritage from generations past to pass along to your children, you are blessed. What a marvelous legacy to be able to carry on. Your children will be especially suited to grow in the things of the Lord because of a unique family tradition.

Perhaps you do not have a heritage of Christianity in your family. Maybe you are the first Christian or one of the only Christians in your family. Then the spiritual heritage begins with you! One hundred years from now, you will be the great-great-grandmother who began the legacy of Christianity in your family. Never underestimate the influence of *one* Christian on many generations to come. You and your children can be the ones who pass it on.

Heavenly Father,
Thank You for a legacy of Christianity. Whether it has
been a part of my family for generations or whether it
is starting with me, may I be faithful in passing on a
spiritual inheritance to my children. Help me to see every
day as the continuation of the process of molding future
generations. Amen.

Come Home, It's Suppertime

Better is a dinner of herbs where love is,
Than a fatted calf with hatred.

PROVERBS 15:17

Some of my favorite childhood memories center around the dinner table. My parents insisted we eat dinner together as a family. I remember the happy feeling of being outside on a hot summer evening in Florida and hearing Mom call outside to us, saying it was time to eat. We would (usually) drop whatever we were doing and make a beeline for the house, in part because we were hungry, and also because it was air-conditioned inside.

Sitting down to dinner was like opening a treasure chest, because we never knew what was awaiting us. It was also one time in my life when I could eat until I couldn't hold another bite, drink a big glass of *whole* milk, have some dessert and never gain an ounce. Truly the "good ol' days."

There were also the occasions when the extended family would join us for dinner. Having grandparents, aunts, uncles and cousins around the table was an especially fun time. Sure there were those occasions when one of the kids refused to eat the required vegetables, and a battle of the wills occurred between parent and child. I remember many an evening when my sister Tina would be at the table long after everyone else was finished because she wasn't allowed to get up until she ate a particularly hated food. She now admits that the dog came in quite handy in these situations.

There were times when my sisters and I were teenagers that this "family eats together" rule became an obstacle to us, but I realize now that Mom and Dad weren't trying to ruin our social lives; they had long-term goals in mind. They wanted us to learn to communicate and share experiences as a family rather than constantly go our own ways.

In their book *Common Sense Parenting*, Kent and Barbara Hughes say that establishing a dinnertime routine promotes what they call "family affection." They write:

> Family affection is not the same as family love. Most people have the commonsense knowledge which says we are supposed to love our family members.... This kind of love springs from a sense of loyalty and duty. Family affection, on the other hand, involves genuinely *liking* each other—you actually enjoy being together.

As a result of our experiences with family dinnertime, Gary and I have made having dinner together a priority in our marriage. At first we would occasionally gravitate to eating dinner on trays in front of the television. But we noticed that it put an end to any sort of meaningful conversation, so we began to make an effort not to eat in front of the tube.

Right now we are in the stage of teaching manners and dealing with messy hands and faces, and with food that ends up on the floor almost as often as it makes it into a little mouth. But we believe that someday we will begin to see the fruits of our labor when dinner becomes an anticipated event of conversation and communication. Even though our son is only three, we already have talks about what he did during the day and our plans for the rest of the night; and we look forward to future happenings.

We want to promote family affection. Both Gary and I enjoyed it with our families, and our parents didn't even have a specific term to identify what they were doing. A dinnertime tradition is one we intend to continue in our own family—because we really do *like* each other, and we want it to stay this way!

The more a child becomes aware of a mother's willingness to listen, the more a mother will begin to hear.

Anonymous

Heavenly Father,
Help me build a tradition of communication and conversation within my family. May our mealtimes become a time of sharing and learning about each other. Whether we are two or ten in number, thank You for the blessing of being a part of a family. Amen.

Family Prayer

Then he spoke a parable to them, that men always ought to pray and not lose heart.

LUKE 18:1

I have some special memories associated with prayer. My first memory is of my dad coming into the bedroom every night after my sisters and I had gone to bed, to pray with us. Dad would always have had some kind of "snack" beforehand, so his breath would often reek of onions or peanut butter or something equally strong. He got a big kick out of his three girls shrieking about his bad breath as he got right down in our faces for prayer!

My most treasured "prayer memory" is of Little Gary saying his first prayer at the age of seventeen months. He said, "G-us, I-U. Amen." (Translation: *Jesus, I love You. Amen.*) My heart soared as he said a prayer that only a mother, father and Jesus could understand.

We have made it a priority to pray together as a family. We pray after we have devotions every night with Little Gary, and I'm always proud of the prayer requests that my son suggests. He doesn't know it yet, but he's already praying about *everything*, just like Philippians 4:6 says to do.

For Gary and me, praying together as a couple has been more of a challenge and requires discipline. Not because we don't want to pray together, but we have a hard time deciding *when* to pray. Gary likes to pray like Paul and Silas ...at midnight! By that time I'm exhausted; I prefer to get up early and have my time of Bible study and prayer. Unfortunately, my night-owl husband can't think, let alone study or pray, before noon. So we have to compromise and come up with suitable alternatives.

I keep a journal of things that I read and study that are of special importance to me. My journal is full of Scripture verses, quotations and passages from books and other sources. I also keep our prayer lists in my journal. In looking back over the prayer lists of the last two years, I was amazed at the answers to prayer that we have received. I don't know why I was amazed because we are promised answers to our prayers (see Matthew 21:22), but to see our requests in writing, then to see the answers to each one, is inspiring.

As parents, we have a lot to pray about. Praying for our children is one of our greatest parental responsibilities. Praying for their salvation, knowledge of right and wrong, safety and development should be a joy. What an awesome thought to know that God hears and answers our prayers! Even the ones, or maybe especially the ones, that come from the mouths of babes.

Heavenly Father,
Teach me the importance of prayer that I may pass
that knowledge to my children. As I tell You my deepest
thoughts, fears and desires in prayer, allow me to hear
Your voice speaking to me in return. May I find Your will
for my life as I learn to listen to You. Amen.

Epilogue

I hope that you have enjoyed reading *Dreams I'm Dreamin'*. Maybe you have laughed. Or maybe you have cried. My biggest wish, however, is that you have been encouraged to take on the job of motherhood with passion, confidence and enthusiasm. Rose Kennedy once said:

I looked on child rearing not only as a work of love and duty but as a profession that was fully as interesting and challenging as any honorable profession in the world and one that demanded the best that I could bring to it.

Being a mother is certainly a challenge, one that we should strive to meet with our very best efforts. There is much to teach and much to learn. There is much to do for our children, and there is much to allow them to do for themselves.

All the demands on your time and energy can be overwhelming, I know. So I want to close this book by reminding you of the single most important thing you can ever do for your children—pursue your own personal relationship with Jesus Christ. If we strive to have a vital relationship with our Lord, then we will be refreshed in our spirits and able to deal with the rest of life's challenges.

In the inspiring book *Beauty to Ashes*, Zac Poonen writes:

What God has begun in us He will complete. As perfect as was the work of the Father in creation and as perfect as was the work of the Son in our redemption, so perfect will the work of the Holy Spirit be in our sanctification. God is faithful.

Acknowledgements

The publisher and author wish to thank the following individuals and organizations for their cooperation in the completion of this project.

Dreams I'm Dreamin'

"Dreams I'm Dreamin'" is featured on the Warner Alliance Records album *By Faith*, by Kim Boyce. Lyrics by Kim Boyce. Music by Bo Cooper. © 1994 Sunday Shoes Music, HOWLIN' HITS/KOREIBA MUSIC/ASCAP. All rights reserved. Used by permission of Benson Music Group, Inc., Nashville, TN.

Amazing Love for Me

"Amazing Love for Me" is featured on the Diadem/Benson album *As I Am*, by Kim Boyce. Lyrics by Kim Boyce, Tony Wood and Scott Krippayne. ©1997 Diadem Sky/Kim Boyce Music/ASCAP, BMG SONGS, INC./ABOVE THE RIM MUSIC/ASCAP. All rights reserved. Used by permission of Benson Music Group, Inc.

"Who Hung the Moon?" is featured on the Diadem/Benson album *As I Am*, by Kim Boyce. Lyrics by Bo Cooper and Todd Cooper. © 1997 Sunday Shoes Music/ASCAP, SAFE SAX/BMI. All rights reserved. Used by permission of Benson Music Group, Inc.

"Vibia Perpetua" excerpt from *Great Women of the Christian Faith* by Edith Deen. © 1959 by Edith Deen. Published by Barbour and Company, Inc. All rights reserved.

Let's Stay Together

"Let's Stay Together" is featured on the Warner Alliance Records album *Facts of Love*, by Kim Boyce. Lyrics by Kim Boyce and Gary Koreiba. Music by Phil Sillas. © 1992 HOWLIN' HITS/KOREIBA MUSIC/ASCAP/Word Music (a division of WORD MUSIC) ASCAP. Used by permission. All rights reserved.

Epilogue

CORRESPONDENCE:

Kim Boyce Ministries
200 Nathan Dr.
Hollister, MO 65672

Printed in the United States
87163LV00009B/2/A